ITALIAN COOKING 2021 VOL. 3

HEALTHY SALADS

Martha Rossi

How do you eat healthy?

People often think of healthy eating as dieting. This is not true. Eating healthy is not just about losing weight, it's about feeling better both physically and mentally. Eating healthy is about balance and making sure that your body is getting the necessary nutrients it needs to function properly. Healthy eating habits require that people eat fruits, vegetables, whole grains, fats, proteins, and starches. Keep in mind that healthy eating requires that you're mindful of what you eat and drink, but also how you prepare it. For best results, individuals should avoid fried or processed foods, as well as foods high in added sugars and salts.

The fundamentals of healthy eating

While some extreme diets may suggest otherwise, we all need a balance of protein, fat, carbohydrates, fiber, vitamins, and minerals in our diets to sustain a healthy body. You don't need to eliminate certain categories of food from your diet, but rather select the healthiest options from each category.

Top 5 Benefits of Healthy Eating

- Weight loss
- Heart Health
- Strong bones and teeth
- Better mood and energy levels
- Improved memory and brain health

Switching to a healthy diet doesn't have to be an all or nothing proposition. You don't have to be perfect, you don't have to completely eliminate foods you enjoy, and you don't have to change everything all at once—that usually only leads to cheating or giving up on your new eating plan.

To set yourself up for success, try to keep things simple. Eating a healthier diet doesn't have to be complicated.Focus on avoiding packaged and processed foods and opting for more fresh ingredients whenever possible.

- Prepare more of your own meals
- Make the right changes
- Read the labels
- Focus on how you feel after eating
- Drink plenty of water

Now that you have all the information you need to start; you just need willpower and perseverance to improve your life in a meaningful way. Just by changing your meal plan with a healthier one, eating more various and, more important, enjoying your daily life, you will notice big changes in your life and that of your loved ones.

ITALIAN HOME COOKING

MARTHA ROSSI

Quick and easy recipes from the Italian cuisine for your complete Mediterranean diet. Learn how to combine fresh and low-budget ingredients, to prepare healthy but delicious salads!

This cookbook is suitable for beginners.

HEALTHY SALADS

ITALIAN HOME COOKING SERIES
VOLUME 3 HEALTHY SALADS

ITALIAN HOME COOKING V. 1

Soups and stews. Quick and easy recipes from the Italian cuisine for your complete Mediterranean diet! Learn how to combine fresh and low-budget ingredients, to cook healthy but delicious soups and stews! This cookbook is suitable for beginners.

ITALIAN HOME COOKING V. 2

Quick and easy recipes from Italy. This second volume will walk you through yummy and low--budget recipes ideal for weight loss and workout. With healthy salads and bowls recipes that come directly from the Mediterranean diet, learn how to lose weight and cook some of the best salads ideas for a good life! This cookbook is suitable for beginners.

ITALIAN HOME COOKING V. 3

Quick and easy recipes from the Italian cuisine for your complete Mediterranean diet. Learn how to combine fresh and low-budget ingredients, to prepare healthy but delicious salads! This cookbook is suitable for beginners.

ITALIAN HOME COOKING V. 4

Quick-and-easy recipes from Italy! Build your complete Mediterranean meal plan for a diet that helps you lose weight, while still eating your favourite seafood! Learn how to combine fresh ingredients with this new cookbook, suitable for beginners.

ITALIAN HOME COOKING V. 5

Time saving recipes from the Italian cuisine for a healthy Mediterranean diet! Learn how to properly cook poultry and build a complete meal plan! This cookbook is suitable for beginners and contains low-budget and quick recipes.

ITALIAN HOME COOKING V. 6

Quick-and-easy recipes from the Italian cuisine to set up your complete Mediterranean diet. Learn how to cook pasta and build a delicious and healthy meal plan! This cookbook is suitable for beginners and contains low-budget and time saving ideas.

ITALIAN HOME COOKING V. 7

Time saving recipes from Italy for a healthy and complete Mediterranean diet! Learn how to properly cook delicious smoothies for your breakfast with fruit and a variety of different ingredients! This cookbook is suitable for beginners.

ITALIAN RECIPES FOR BEGINNERS 2021

2 books in 1: Italian Home Cooking fish and Pasta! This cookbook contains simple but classy meals to prepare step-by-step, perfect for your home cooking, parties or aperitifs either. Lose weight by eating well with the right recipe book, for a complete and time-saving Mediterranean diet!

MEDITERRANEAN DIET COOKBOOK ITALY

If you want to eat healthy italian recipes, but you don't know where to start... This recipe book for beginners will show you some of the best ideas to prepare Delicious breakfast, salads, poultry, soups and stews, which are ideal for your weight loss meal plan!

Table of Contents

YOUR COLOURED
HEALTHY CHOICE

Rosemary Carrots and Onion Mix

Preparation time: 5 mins - **Cooking time:** 25 mins -
N. servings: 4

Ingredients:

- 1 onion.
- 1 tablespoon olive oil.
- 1 pound carrots, peeled and roughly sliced.
- 1 orange, peeled and cut into segments.
- Juice of 1 orange.
- 1 tablespoon rosemary, chopped.
- Zest of 1 orange, grated.
- A pinch of salt and black pepper.

Procedures:

1. Heat up a pan with the oil over medium-high heat, add the onion and sauté for 5 mins;

2. Add the carrots, the orange zest and the other ingredients, toss, cook over medium heat for 25 mins.

3. Divide between plates and serve it;

Nutrition facts per serving: calories 140 - fat 3.9 - fiber 5 - carbs 26.1 - protein 2.1

Zucchini and Apples Mix

Ingredients:

- 2 apples, peeled, cored and cubed.
- 2 tablespoons olive oil.
- 1 tablespoon chives, chopped.
- 1 yellow onion, chopped.
- 1 pound zucchinis, sliced.
- 1 tomato, cubed.
- 1 tablespoon rosemary, chopped.

Procedures:

1. Heat up a pan with the oil over medium heat, add the onion and sauté for 5 mins;
2. Add the zucchinis and the other ingredients, toss and cook over medium heat for 20 min.
3. Divide between plates and serve it as a side dish;

Nutrition facts per serving: calories 170 - fat 5 - fiber 2 - carbs 11 - protein 7

Bell Peppers and Scallions Mix

Preparation time: 5 mins - **Cooking time:** 20 mins -
N. servings: 4

Ingredients:

- 1 yellow bell pepper, cut into strips.
- 1 red bell pepper, cut into strips.
- 1 orange bell pepper, cut into strips.
- 1 tablespoon olive oil.
- 1 tablespoon coconut aminos.
- 1 green bell pepper, cut into strips.
- 3 scallions, chopped.
- A pinch of salt and black pepper.
- 1 tablespoon rosemary, chopped.
- 1 tablespoon parsley, chopped.

Procedures:

1. Heat up a pan with the oil over medium-high heatadd the scallions and sauté for 5 mins;
2. Add the bell peppers and the other ingredients, toss, cook over medium heat for 17 min, divide between plates and serve it;

Nutrition facts per serving: calories 120 - fat 1- fiber 2- carbs 7- protein 6

Black Beans and Peppers Mix

Preparation time: 10 mins - **Cooking time:** 20 mins - **N. servings:** 4

Ingredients:

- 2 cups black beans, cooked and drained.
- 1 green bell pepper, chopped.
- 4 garlic cloves, minced.
- 1 tablespoon olive oil.
- 1 yellow onion, chopped.
- 1 teaspoon cumin, ground.
- 1/2 cup chicken stock.
- A pinch of salt and black pepper.
- 1 tablespoon coriander, chopped.

Procedures:

1. Heat up a pan with the oil over medium heat, add the onion and the garlic and sauté for 5 mins at least;
2. Add the black beans and the other ingredients, toss, cook over medium heat for 20 mins, divide between plates and serve it;

Nutrition facts per serving: calories 221- fat 5 - fiber 4 - carbs 9 - protein 11

Chili and Dill Cucumber Mix

Preparation time: 10 mins - **Cooking time:** 0 mins - **N. servings:** 4

Ingredients:

- 1 pound cucumbers, sliced.
- 1 tablespoon olive oil.
- 1 teaspoon chili powder.
- 1 garlic clove, minced.
- 1 tablespoon balsamic vinegar.
- 1 green chili, chopped.
- 1 tablespoon dill, chopped.
- 2 tablespoons lime juice.

Procedures:

1. In a bowl, combine the cucumbers with the garlic, the oil and the other ingredients, toss and serve it as a side salad;

Nutrition facts per serving: calories 132 - fat 3 - fiber 1 -carbs 7 - protein 4

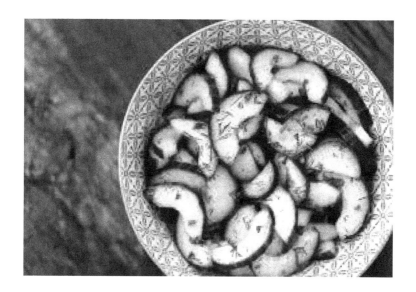

Lime Tomato Salad

Preparation time: 10 mins - **Cooking time:** 0 mins - **N. servings:** 4

Ingredients:

- 1 pound cherry tomatoes, halved.
- 3 scallions, chopped.
- 1 tablespoon olive oil.
- 1 tablespoon lime juice.
- A pinch of salt and black pepper.
- 1/4 cup parsley, chopped.

Procedures:

1. In a bowl, combine the tomatoes with the scallions and the other ingredients
2. Toss and serve it as a side salad;

Nutrition facts per serving: calories 180 - fat 2 - fiber 2 - carbs 8 - protein 6

Chickpeas and Capers Salad

Preparation time: 5 mins - **Cooking time:** 0 mins - **N. servings:** 4

Ingredients:

- 2 tablespoons olive oil.
- 4 spring onions, chopped.
- 2 cups chickpeas, cooked.
- 1 tablespoon capers, chopped.
- 2 tablespoons lime juice.
- 1 teaspoon chili powder.
- 1 teaspoon cumin, ground.
- 1 tablespoon parsley, chopped.
- A pinch of salt and black pepper.

Procedures:

1. In a bowl, combine the chickpeas with the capers and the other ingredients, toss and serve it as a side salad;

Nutrition facts per serving: calories 212 - fat 4 - fiber 4 - carbs 12 - protein 6

Cucumber Salad

Preparation time: 5 mins - **Cooking time:** 0 mins - **N. servings:** 4

Ingredients:

- 1/2 cup cilantro, chopped.
- 4 spring onions, chopped.
- 2 tablespoons olive oil.
- 2 cucumbers, sliced.
- 1/2 cup lemon juice.
- Salt and black pepper to the taste.

Procedures:

1. In a salad bowl, combine the cucumbers with the spring onions and the other ingredients
2. Toss and serve it;

Nutrition facts per serving: calories 163 - fat 1 - fiber 2 - carbs 7 - protein 9

Mango and Spring Onions Mix

Preparation time: 5 mins - **Cooking time:** 0 mins - **N. servings:** 4

Ingredients:

- 2 spring onions, chopped.
- 1 avocado, peeled, pitted and cubed.
- 2 mangos, peeled and chopped.
- 1 tablespoon oregano, chopped.
- Salt and black pepper to the taste.
- 1 tablespoon olive oil.
- 1 tablespoon chives, chopped.
- 1 tablespoon basil, chopped.
- 2 tablespoons lemon juice.

Procedures:

1. In a salad bowl, mix the mangos with the spring onions, the avocado and the other ingredients.

2. Toss and serve it as a side dish;

Nutrition facts per serving: calories 200 - fat 5 - fiber 7, - carbs 12 - protein 3

Cabbage and Dates Salad

Preparation time: 10 mins - **Cooking time:** 0 mins -
N. servings: 4

Ingredients:

- 2 cups green cabbage, shredded.
- 4 dates, chopped.
- 2 tablespoons walnuts, chopped.
- 1 carrot, grated.
- 1 tablespoon apple cider vinegar.
- 3 tablespoons olive oil.
- 1 tablespoon parsley, chopped.
- 1 tablespoon lemon juice.
- 2 garlic cloves, minced.
- A pinch of salt and black pepper.

Procedures:

1. In a bowl, combine the cabbage with the carrots, dates and the other ingredients.
2. Toss and serve it as a side salad;

Nutrition facts per serving: calories 140 - fat 3, fiber 4 - carbs 5 - protein 14

Orange Cucumber Salad

Preparation time: 5 mins - **Cooking time:** 0 mins - **N. servings:** 4

Ingredients:

- 1 green apple, cored and cubed.
- 3 spring onions, chopped.
- 2 cucumbers, sliced.
- A pinch of salt and black pepper.
- 3 tablespoons olive oil.
- 4 teaspoons orange juice.
- 1 tablespoon mint, chopped.
- 1 tablespoon lemon juice.

Procedures:

1. In a bowl mix the cucumbers with the apple, spring onions and the other ingredients. Toss and serve it as a side salad;

Nutrition facts per serving: calories 110 - fat 0 - fiber 3 - carbs 6 - protein 8

Almond Broccoli Mix

Preparation time: 10 mins - **Cooking time:** 20 mins -
N. servings: 4

Ingredients:

- 1 cup broccoli florets.
- 1 tablespoon walnuts, chopped.
- 1 tablespoon almonds, chopped.
- 2 tablespoons olive oil.
- 2 endives, shredded.
- 2 garlic cloves, minced.
- 1 teaspoon cumin, ground.
- 1 teaspoon chili powder.
- 1 teaspoon rosemary, dried.

Procedures:

1. In a roasting pan, combine the endives with the broccoli and the other ingredients, toss and bake at 380 degrees F for 25 mins;

2. Divide the mix between plates and serve it;

Nutrition facts per serving: calories 139 - fat 9.8 - fiber 9.3 - carbs 11.9 - protein 4.9

Arugula and Tomato Salad

Preparation time: 5 mins - **Cooking time:** 0 mins - **N. servings:** 4

Ingredients:

- 2 cups baby arugula.
- 1/2 cup cherry tomatoes, halved.
- 1 tablespoon olive oil.
- Juice of 1 lime.
- 1 tablespoon chives, chopped.
- 1 tablespoon balsamic vinegar.
- A pinch of salt and black pepper.

Procedures:

1. In a bowl, mix the arugula with the lime juice, cherry tomatoes and the other ingredients. Toss and serve it;

Nutrition facts per serving: calories 190 - fat 2 - fiber 6 - carbs 1 – protein 4

Radish and Spring Onions Salad

Preparation time: 10 mins - **Cooking time:** 0 mins - **N. servings:** 4

Ingredients:
- A pinch of salt and black pepper.
- 2 cups radishes, sliced.
- 2 spring onions, chopped.
- 2 tablespoons balsamic vinegar.
- 1 tablespoon chives, chopped.
- 1 teaspoon rosemary, dried.
- 2 tablespoons olive oil.

Procedures:
1. In a salad bowl, mix the radishes with the spring onions, salt, pepper and the rest, toss and serve it as a side salad;

Nutrition facts per serving: calories 110 - fat 4 - fiber 2 - carbs 7 - protein 7

Lemon and Chives Tomato Mix

Preparation time: 10 mins - **Cooking time:** 0 mins - **N. servings:** 4

Ingredients:

- 3 celery stalks, chopped.
- 1 tablespoon chives, chopped.
- 1 pound cherry tomatoes, halved.
- 2 spring onions, chopped.
- A pinch of sea salt and black pepper.
- Juice of 1 lemon.
- A pinch of cayenne pepper.

Procedures:

1. In a salad bowl, combine the celery with the cherry tomatoes and the other ingredients, toss and serve it as a side dish;

Nutrition facts per serving: calories 80 - fat 3 - fiber 1 - carbs 8 - protein 5

Corn and Spinach Mix

Preparation time: 10 mins - **Cooking time:** 0 mins -
N. servings: 4

Ingredients:

- 1 cup corn.
- 1 avocado, peeled, pitted and cubed.
- 1 tablespoon mint, chopped.
- 1 cup baby spinach.
- Juice of 1 lemon.
- Zest of 1 lemon, grated.
- 1 tablespoon avocado oil.
- A pinch of sea salt and black pepper.

Procedures:

1. In a salad bowl, mix the corn with the avocado, the spinach and the other ingredients, toss and serve it as a side dish;

Nutrition facts per serving: calories 90 - fat 2 - fiber 1 - carbs 7 - protein 5

Quinoa and Cucumber Mix

Preparation time: 10 mins - **Cooking time:** 0 mins -
N. servings: 4

Ingredients:

- 1 cup baby spinach.
- 1 cup quinoa, cooked.
- A pinch of sea salt and black pepper.
- 2 tablespoons balsamic vinegar.
- 2 tablespoons cilantro, chopped.
- 1 cucumber, chopped.
- 1 teaspoon chili powder.

Procedures:

1. In a bowl, mix the quinoa with the spinach and the other ingredients, toss and serve this as a side dish;

Nutrition facts per serving: calories 100 - fat 0.5 - fiber 2 - carbs 6 - protein 6

Chard and Spring Onions Mix

Preparation time: 10 mins I **Cooking time:** 15 mins I
N. servings: 4

Ingredients:

- 2 spring onions, chopped.
- 2 tablespoons olive oil.
- 2 teaspoons ginger, grated.
- 2 tablespoons balsamic vinegar.
- 1/2 teaspoon red pepper flakes, crushed.
- 4 cups red chard, shredded.
- 1 tablespoon chives, chopped.

Procedures:

1. Heat up a pan with the oil over medium heat, add the spring onions and the ginger and sauté for 5 mins;
2. Add the chard and the other ingredients, toss, cook for 10 mins more, divide between plates and serve it as a side dish;

Nutrition facts per serving: calories 160, fat 10, fiber 3, carbs 10, protein 5

Cabbage and Walnuts Mix

Preparation time: 10 mins - **Cooking time:** 0 mins - **N. servings:** 4

Ingredients:

- 2 tablespoons walnuts, chopped.
- 1 bunch green onions, chopped.
- 1 cup green cabbage, shredded.
- 1 cup tomatoes, cubed.
- 1/4 cup balsamic vinegar.
- 2 tablespoons olive oil.
- 1 tablespoon chives, chopped.
- A pinch of salt and black pepper.

Procedures:

1. In a salad bowl, mix the cabbage with the tomatoes, the walnuts and the other ingredients, toss and serve it as a side dish;

Nutrition facts per serving: calories 140 - fat 3 - fiber 3 - carbs 8 - protein 6

Balsamic Carrots and Scallions Salad

Preparation time: 10 mins - **Cooking time:** 0 mins - **N. servings:** 4

Ingredients:

- 3 scallions, chopped.
- 1 pound carrots, peeled and sliced.
- 1/2 cup cilantro, chopped.
- 3 tablespoons sesame seeds.
- 2 tablespoons balsamic vinegar.
- 2 tablespoons olive oil.
- A pinch of salt and black pepper.

Procedures:

1. In a salad bowl, mix the carrots with the scallions and the other ingredients, toss well and serve it as a side dish;

Nutrition facts per serving: calories 140 - fat 4 - fiber 3 - carbs 5 - protein 6

Sweet Potatoes and Walnuts Mix

Preparation time: 10 mins - **Cooking time:** 30 mins - **N. servings:** 4

Ingredients:

- 2 sweet potatoes, peeled and cut into wedges.
- 2 garlic cloves, minced.
- 2 tablespoons raisins.
- Juice of 1/2 lemon.
- 2 tablespoons walnuts, chopped.
- A pinch of salt and black pepper.
- 2 tablespoons olive oil.

Procedures:

1. In a roasting pan, combine the sweet potatoes with the raisins and the other ingredients, toss and bake at 360 degrees F for 25 mins;
2. Divide everything between plates and serve it;

Nutrition facts per serving: calories 120 - fat 1 - fiber 2 - carbs 3 - protein 5

Radish Salad

Preparation time: 10 mins I **Cooking time:** 0 mins I
N. servings: 4

Ingredients:

- 2 cups green cabbage, shredded.
- 1/2 cup radishes, sliced.
- 1 tablespoon olive oil.
- 4 scallions, chopped.
- A pinch of salt and black pepper.
- 1 tablespoon chives, chopped.
- 1 teaspoon sesame seeds.

Procedures:

1. In a bowl, combine the radishes with the cabbage
   and the other ingredients, toss and serve it;

Nutrition facts per serving: calories 121 - fat 3 - fiber
4 - carbs 8.30 - protein 3

Balsamic Squash Mix

Preparation time: 10 mins - **Cooking time:** 25 mins - **N. servings:** 4

Ingredients:

- 1 butternut squash, peeled and roughly cubed.
- 2 spring onions, chopped.
- 1 tablespoon avocado oil.
- 1 tablespoon balsamic vinegar.
- 1 tablespoon cilantro, chopped.
- A pinch of salt and black pepper.
- 1/2 cup pecans, toasted and chopped.

Procedures:

1. In a roasting pan, combine the squash with the spring onions and the other ingredients, toss and bake at 390 degrees F for 27 mins;
2. Divide the mix between plates and serve it;

Nutrition facts per serving: calories 211 - fat 3 - fiber 4 - carbs 9 - protein 6

Cinnamon and Ginger Carrots Mix

Preparation time: 10 mins - **Cooking time:** 30 mins - **N. servings:** 4

Preparation time:

- 1 pound baby carrots, peeled.
- 1 tablespoon ginger, grated.
- 1 tablespoon coconut oil, melted.
- 3 tablespoons cinnamon powder.
- 1 tablespoon chives, chopped.

Procedures:

1. Spread the carrots on a baking sheet lined with parchment paper, add the ginger and the other ingredients, toss and bake at 380 degrees F for 30 mins.
2. Divide everything between plates and serve it.

Nutrition facts per serving: calories 198 - fat 2 - fiber 4 - carbs 11 - protein 6

Rice and Tomato Salad

Preparation time: 10 mins - **Cooking time:** 0 mins - **N. servings:** 4

Ingredients:

- 2 cups brown rice, cooked.
- 2 tablespoons olive oil.
- 1/4 cup cilantro, chopped.
- 1/2 cup cherry tomatoes, halved.
- 2 teaspoons cumin, ground.
- A pinch of salt and black pepper.
- 2 tablespoons olive oil.

Procedures:

1. In a bowl, combine the rice with the oil and the other ingredients, toss and serve it;

Nutrition facts per serving: calories 122 - fat 4 - fiber 3 - carbs 8 - protein 5

Chili Avocado and Onion Salad

Preparation time: 10 mins - **Cooking time:** 0 mins - **N. servings:** 4

Ingredients:

- 2 red onions, sliced.
- 1 tablespoon olive oil.
- 1 tablespoon dill, chopped.
- A pinch of salt and black pepper.
- 2 avocados, peeled, pitted and roughly sliced.
- 1 tablespoon balsamic vinegar.
- 1 teaspoon chili powder.

Procedures:

1. In a bowl, combine the avocado with the onions and the other ingredients.
2. Toss, and serve it;

Nutrition facts per serving: calories 171 - fat 2 - fiber 7 - carbs 13 - protein 6

Garlic Bok Choy Mix

Preparation time: 10 mins - **Cooking time:** 20 mins -
N. servings: 4

Ingredients:

- 1 yellow onion, chopped.
- 1 tablespoon red pepper flakes, crushed.
- 3 garlic cloves, minced. 1 tablespoon olive oil.
- A pinch of salt and black pepper.
- 1 pound bock choy, torn.
- 1/4 cup cilantro, chopped.

Procedures:

1. Heat up a pan with the oil over medium heat, add the onion and the garlic and sauté for at least 5 mins;
2. Add the bock choy and the other ingredients, toss, cook over medium heat for 15 mins, divide between plates. Serve it as a side dish;

Nutrition facts per serving: calories 143 - fat 3 - fiber 4 - carbs 3 - protein 6

Endives Salad

Preparation time: 10 mins - **Cooking time:** 0 mins _
N. servings: 4

Ingredients:

- 2 tablespoons olive oil.
- 2 ounces watercress, chopped.
- 1 tablespoon balsamic vinegar.
- 4 scallions, chopped.
- 2 endives, trimmed and thinly sliced.
- 1 tablespoon tarragon, chopped.
- 1 tablespoon chives, chopped.
- A pinch of salt and black pepper.
- 1 tablespoon pine nuts, toasted.
- 1 tablespoon walnuts, chopped.

Procedures:

1. In a bowl, mix the endives with the scallions, the watercress, the other ingredients, toss well and serve it as a side salad;

Nutrition facts per serving: calories 140 - fat 10.3 - fiber 8.8 - carbs 10.5 - protein 4.8

Cumin Corn Mix

Preparation time: 10 mins - **Cooking time:** 15 mins - **N. servings:** 4

Ingredients:

- 2 zucchinis, roughly sliced.
- 2 tablespoon olive oil.
- 4 green onions, chopped.
- 1 cup corn.
- 1 yellow onion, thinly sliced.
- 2 teaspoons chili paste.
- 1/4 cup vegetable stock.
- 1/2 teaspoon cumin, ground.
- 1 tablespoon rosemary, chopped.

Procedures:

1. Heat up a pan with the oil over medium-high heat, add the onion and the chili paste. Stir and sauté for 5 mins;
2. Add the corn, zucchinis and the other ingredients, toss well, cook over medium heat for 12 min, divide between plates and serve it as a side dish;

Nutrition facts per serving: calories 142 - fat 7 - fiber 4 - carbs 5 - protein 3

Spinach, Cucumber and Pine Nuts Salad

Preparation time: 5 mins - **Cooking time:** 0 mins -
N. servings: 4

Ingredients:

- 1 cucumber, sliced.
- 1 tomato, cubed.
- 1 pound baby spinach.
- 3 tablespoons olive oil.
- A pinch of red pepper, crushed.
- 1 yellow onion, sliced.
- 1/4 cup pine nuts, toasted.
- 2 tablespoons balsamic vinegar.
- A pinch of salt and black pepper.

Procedures:

1. In a large bowl, combine the spinach with the cucumber, tomato and the other ingredients, toss and serve it as a side salad;

Nutrition facts per serving: calories 120 - fat 1 - fiber 2 - carbs 3 - protein 6

Avocado, Arugula and Olives Salad

Preparation time: 5 mins - **Cooking time:** 0 mins - **N. servings:** 4

Ingredients:

- 2 tablespoons olive oil.
- 2 avocados, peeled, pitted and cut into wedges.
- 1 cup kalamata olives, pitted and halved.
- 1 cup tomatoes, cubed.
- 1 tablespoon ginger, grated.
- A pinch of black pepper.
- 2 cups baby arugula.
- 1 tablespoon balsamic vinegar.

Procedures:

1. In a bowl, combine the avocados with the kalamata and the other ingredients, toss and serve it as a side dish;

Nutrition facts per serving: calories 320 - fat 30.4 - fiber 8.7 - carbs 13 - protein 3

Radish and Olives Salad

Preparation time: 5 mins - **Cooking time:** 0 mins - **N. servings:** 4

Ingredients:

- 1 pound radishes, cubed.
- 2 green onions, sliced.
- 2 tablespoons balsamic vinegar.
- 1 teaspoon chili powder.
- 2 tablespoon olive oil.
- 1 cup black olives, pitted and halved.
- A pinch of black pepper.

Procedures:

1. In a salad bowl, combine radishes with the onions and the other ingredients, toss and serve it as a side dish;

Nutrition facts per serving: calories 123 - fat 10.8 - fiber 3.3 -carbs 7 - protein 1.3

Lemony Endives and Cucumber Salad

Preparation time: 5 mins - **Cooking time:** 0 mins -
N. servings: 4

Ingredients:

- 1/4 cup lemon juice.
- 1/4 cup olive oil.
- 2 endives, roughly shredded.
- 1 tablespoon dill, chopped.
- 1 cucumber, sliced.
- 2 cups baby spinach.
- 2 tomatoes, cubed.
- 1/2 cups walnuts, chopped.

Procedures:

1. In a bowl, combine the endives with the spinach and the other ingredients, toss and serve it as a side dish;

Nutrition facts per serving: calories 238 - fat 22.3 - fiber 3.1 - carbs 8.4 - protein 5.7

Jalapeno Corn Mix

Preparation time: 5 mins - **Cooking time:** 0 mins -
N. servings: 4

Ingredients:

- 4 cups corn.
- 1 tablespoon basil, chopped.
- 1 tablespoon balsamic vinegar.
- A pinch of black pepper.
- 2 cups black olives, pitted and halved.
- 1 red onion, chopped.
- 2 cups romaine lettuce, shredded.
- 1/2 cup cherry tomatoes, halved.
- 1 tablespoon jalapeno, chopped.
- 2 tablespoons olive oil.

Procedures:

1. In a bowl, combine the corn with the olives, lettuce and the other ingredients, toss well, divide between plates. serve it as a side dish;

Nutrition facts per serving: calories 290 - fat 16.1 - fiber 7.4 - carbs 37.6 - protein 6.27

Arugula and Pomegranate Salad

Preparation time: 5 mins - **Cooking time:** 0 mins - **N. servings:** 4

Ingredients:

- 1 tablespoon balsamic vinegar.
- 1/2 shallot, chopped.
- 5 cups baby arugula.
- 1/4 cup pomegranate seeds.
- 6 tablespoons green onions, chopped.
- 2 tablespoons olive oil.
- 3 tablespoons pine nuts.

Procedures:

1. In a salad bowl, combine the arugula with the pomegranate and the other ingredients, toss and serve it;

Nutrition facts per serving: calories 120 - fat 11.6 - fiber 0.9 - carbs 4.2 - protein 1.8

Spinach Mix

Preparation time: 10 mins - **Cooking time:** 0 mins -
N. servings: 4

Ingredients:

- 2 tablespoons olive oil.
- 3 cups baby spinach.
- 1/4 cup almonds, toasted and chopped.
- 1 tablespoon lemon juice.
- 2 avocados, peeled, pitted and cut into wedges.
- 1 tablespoon cilantro, chopped.

Procedures:

1. In a bowl, combine the avocados with the almonds, spinach and the other ingredients, toss and serve it as a side dish;

Nutrition facts per serving: calories 181 - fat 4 - fiber 4.8 - carbs 11.4 - protein 6

Green Beans and Lettuce Salad

Preparation time: 4 mins - **Cooking time:** 0 mins - **N. servings:** 4

Ingredients:

- Juice of 1 lime.
- 2 cups romaine lettuce, shredded.
- 1 cup corn.
- 1/2 pound of green beans, blanched and halved.
- 1 cucumber, chopped.
- 1/3 cup chives, chopped.

Procedures:

- In a bowl, combine the green beans with the corn and the other ingredients, toss and serve it;

Nutrition facts per serving: calories 225 - fat 12 - fiber 2.4 - carbs 11.2 - protein 3.5

Endives and Onion Salad

Preparation time: 4 mins - **Cooking time:** 0 mins -
N. servings: 4

Ingredients:

- 2 endives, trimmed and shredded.
- 2 tablespoons lime juice.
- 1 tablespoon balsamic vinegar.
- 1 tablespoon lime zest.
- 3 tablespoons olive oil.
- pound kale, torn.
- 1 red onion, sliced.
- A pinch of black pepper.

Procedures:

1. In a large bowl, combine the endives with the kale and the other ingredients, toss well and serve it cold as a side salad;

Nutrition facts per serving: calories 270 - fat 11.4 - fiber 5 - carbs 14.3 - protein 5.7

Grapes and Spinach Salad

Preparation time: 5 mins - **Cooking time:** 0 mins -
N. servings: 4

Ingredients:

- 2 avocados, peeled, pitted and roughly cubed.
- 1 cucumber, sliced.
- 2 cups baby spinach.
- 2 tablespoons avocado oil.
- 1 and 1/2 cups green grapes, halved.
- 1 tablespoon cider vinegar.
- A pinch of black pepper.
- 2 tablespoons parsley, chopped.

Procedures:

1. In a salad bowl, combine the baby spinach with the avocados and the other ingredients, toss and serve it;

Nutrition facts per serving: calories 277 - fat 11.4 - fiber 5 - carbs 14.6 - protein 4

Parmesan Eggplant Mix

Preparation time: 10 mins - **Cooking time:** 20 mins - **N. servings:** 4

Ingredients:

- 1 tablespoon oregano, chopped.
- 1/2 cup parmesan, grated.
- 2 big eggplants, roughly cubed.
- 2 tablespoons olive oil.
- 1/4 teaspoon garlic powder.
- A pinch of black pepper.

Procedures:

1. In a baking pan combine the eggplants with the oregano and the other ingredients (except the cheese) and toss;
2. Sprinkle parmesan on top, introduce in the oven and bake at 360 degrees F for 22 mins;
3. Divide between plates and serve it as a side dish;

Nutrition facts per serving: calories 248 - fat 8.4 - fiber 4 - carbs 14.3 - protein 5.4

Parmesan Garlic Tomatoes Mix

Preparation time: 10 mins - **Cooking time:** 20 mins - **N. servings:** 4

Ingredients:

- 1 tablespoon basil, chopped.
- 2 pounds tomatoes, halved.
- 3 tablespoons olive oil.
- 1/4 cup parmesan, grated.
- A pinch of black pepper.
- Zest of 1 lemon, grated.
- 3 garlic cloves, minced.

Procedures:

1. In a baking pan, combine the tomatoes with the basil and the other ingredients except the cheese and toss;

2. Sprinkle the parmesan on top and then introduce in the oven at 375 degrees F for 20 mins. Divide between plates and serve it as a side dish;

Nutrition facts per serving: calories 224 - fat 12 - fiber 4.3 - carbs 10.8 - protein 5.1

Corn and Shallots Mix

Preparation time: 10 mins - **Cooking time:** 15 mins - **N. servings:** 4

Ingredients:

- 4 cups corn.
- 1 tablespoon avocado oil.
- 2 shallots, chopped.
- A pinch of black pepper.
- 1 teaspoon chili powder.
- 2 tablespoons tomato pasta.
- 3 scallions, chopped.

Procedures:

1. Heat up a pan with the oil over medium heat, add the scallions and chili powder. Stir and sauté for 5 mins;
2. Add the corn and the other ingredients, toss, cook for 12 mins, divide between plates and serve it as a side dish;

Nutrition facts per serving: calories 259 - fat 11.1 - fiber 2.6 - carbs 13.2 - protein 3.5

Spinach, Almonds and Capers Salad

Preparation time: 10 mins - **Cooking time:** 0 mins - **N. servings:** 4

Ingredients:

- 4 cups baby spinach.
- 1 tablespoon olive oil.
- 1 tablespoon capers.
- 1 cup mango, peeled and cubed.
- 2 spring onions, chopped.
- 1 tablespoon lemon juice.
- 1/3 cup almonds, chopped.

Procedures:

1. In a bowl, mix the spinach and the mango and the other ingredients, toss and serve it;

Nutrition facts per serving: calories 200 - fat 7.4 - fiber 3 - carbs 4.7 - protein 4.4

Carrots and Onion Mix

Preparation time: 10 mins I **Cooking time:** 30 mins I
N. servings: 4

Ingredients:

- 2 tablespoons olive oil.
- 1 pound carrots, peeled and roughly cubed.
- 1 tablespoon sage, chopped.
- 2 teaspoons sweet paprika.
- 1 red onion, chopped.
- A pinch of black pepper.

Procedures:

1. In a baking pan, combine the carrots, the oil and the other ingredients, toss and bake at 390 degrees F for 30 mins;
2. Divide between plates and serve it;

Nutrition facts per serving: calories 200, fat 8.7, fiber 2.5, carbs 7.9, protein 4

Tomatoes and Vinegar Mix

Preparation time: 5 mins - **Cooking time:** 0 mins - **N. servings:** 4

Ingredients:

- 2 tablespoons mint, chopped.
- 1 tablespoon rosemary vinegar
- 2 cups corn.
- 1 pound tomatoes, cut into wedges.
- A pinch of black pepper.
- 2 tablespoons olive oil.

Procedures:

1. In a salad bowl, combine the tomatoes with the corn and the other ingredients, toss and serve it;

Nutrition facts per serving: calories 230 - fat 7.2 - fiber 2 - carbs 11.6 - protein 4

Caraway Cabbage Mix

Preparation time: 5 mins - **Cooking time:** 0 mins -
N. servings: 4

Ingredients:

- 2 green apples, cored and cubed.
- 1 red cabbage head, shredded.
- 2 tablespoons balsamic vinegar.
- 1/2 teaspoon caraway seeds.
- 2 tablespoons olive oil.
- Black pepper to the taste.

Procedures:

1. In a bowl, combine the cabbage with the apples and the other ingredients, toss and serve it as a side salad;

Nutrition facts per serving: calories 165 - fat 7.4 - fiber 7.3 - carbs 26 - protein 2.6

Cabbage and Shallots Salad

Preparation time: 5 mins - **Cooking time:** 0 mins - **N. servings:** 4

Ingredients:

- 2 carrots, grated.
- 1 big red cabbage head, shredded.
- 1 tablespoon red vinegar.
- 2 shallots, chopped.
- 1 tablespoon olive oil.
- A pinch of black pepper.
- 1 tablespoon lime juice.

Procedures:

1. In a bowl, mix the cabbage with the shallots and the other ingredients, toss and serve it as a side salad;

Nutrition facts per serving: calories 106 - fat 3.8 - fiber 6.5 - carbs 18 - protein 3.3

Tomato Salad

Preparation time: 10 mins - **Cooking time:** 0 mins - **N. servings:** 6

Ingredients:

- 1 pound cherry tomatoes, halved.
- A pinch of black pepper.
- 2 tablespoons olive oil.
- 1 tablespoon balsamic vinegar.
- 1 cup kalamata olives, pitted and halved.
- 1 red onion, chopped.
- 1/4 cup cilantro, chopped.

Procedures:

1. In a bowl, mix the tomatoes with the olives and the other ingredients, toss and serve it as a side salad;

Nutrition facts per serving: calories 131 - fat 10.9 - fiber 3.1 - carbs 9.2 - protein 1.6

Pesto Zucchini Salad

Preparation time: 4 mins - **Cooking time:** 0 mins - **N. servings:** 4

Ingredients:

- 1 red onion, sliced.
- 2 zucchinis, cut with a spiralizer.
- 1 tablespoon lemon juice.
- 1 tablespoon basil pesto.
- 1 tablespoon olive oil.
- Black pepper to the taste.
- 1/2 cup cilantro, chopped.

Procedures:

1. In a large salad bowl, mix the zucchinis with the onion and the other ingredients, toss and serve it;

Nutrition facts per serving: calories 58 - fat 3.8 - fiber 1.8 - carbs 6 - protein 1.6

Lettuce Salad

Preparation time: 5 mins - **Cooking time:** 0 mins - **N. servings:** 4

Ingredients:

- 2 garlic cloves, minced.
- 1 tablespoon ginger, grated.
- 4 cups romaine lettuce, torn.
- 1 tablespoon balsamic vinegar.
- 1 beet, peeled and grated.
- 2 green onions, chopped.
- 1 tablespoon sesame seeds.

Procedures:

1. In a bowl, combine the lettuce with the ginger, garlic and the other ingredients. Toss and serve it as a side dish;

Nutrition facts per serving: calories 42 - fat 1.4 - fiber 1.5 - carbs 6.7 - protein 1.4

Black Beans and Shallots Mix

Preparation time: 4 mins - **Cooking time:** 0 mins - **N. servings:** 4

Ingredients:

- 3 cups black beans, cooked.
- 1 cup cherry tomatoes, halved.
- 2 shallots, chopped.
- 3 tablespoons olive oil.
- 1 tablespoon balsamic vinegar.
- Black pepper to the taste.
- 1 tablespoon chives, chopped.

Procedures:

1. In a bowl, combine the beans with the tomatoes and the other ingredients, toss and serve it cold as a side dish;

Nutrition facts per serving: calories 310 - fat 11.0 - fiber 5.3 - carbs 19.6 - protein 6.8

Cilantro Olives Mix

Preparation time: 4 mins - **Cooking time:** 0 mins -
N. servings: 4

Ingredients:
- 2 spring onions, chopped.
- 2 endives, shredded.
- 1 cup black olives, pitted and sliced.
- 1/2 cup kalamata olives, pitted and sliced.
- 1/4 cup apple cider vinegar.
- 2 tablespoons olive oil.
- 1 tablespoons cilantro, chopped.

Procedures:
1. In a bowl, mix the endives with the olives and the other ingredients, toss and serve it.

Nutrition facts per serving: calories 230 - fat 9.1 -
fiber 6.3 - carbs 14.6 - protein 7.2

Basil Tomatoes and Cucumber Mix

Preparation time: 5 mins - **Cooking time:** 0 mins - **N. servings:** 4

Ingredients:

- 1 tablespoon olive oil.
- 2 spring onions, chopped.
- 1/2 pound tomatoes, cubed.
- 2 cucumber, sliced.
- 1/2 cup basil, chopped.
- Black pepper to the taste.
- Juice of 1 lime.

Procedures:

1. In a salad bowl, combine the tomatoes with the cucumber and the other ingredients. Toss and serve it cold;

Nutrition facts per serving: calories 224 - fat 11.2 - fiber 5.1 - carbs 8.9 - protein 6.2

Peppers Salad

Ingredients:

- 1 yellow bell pepper, chopped.
- 1 red bell pepper, chopped.
- 1 cup cherry tomatoes, halved.
- 3 tablespoons red wine vinegar.
- 1 green bell pepper, chopped.
- 1/2 pound carrots, shredded.
- 2 tablespoons olive oil
- Black pepper to the taste.
- 1 tablespoon cilantro, chopped.

Procedures:

1. In a salad bowl, mix the tomatoes with the peppers, carrots and the other ingredients, toss and serve it as a side salad;

Nutrition facts per serving: calories 123 - fat 4 - fiber 8.4 - carbs 14.4 - protein 1.1

Thyme Rice Mix

Preparation time: 10 mins - **Cooking time:** 30 mins - **N. servings:** 4

Ingredients:

- 1 yellow onion, chopped.
- 2 tablespoons olive oil.
- 2 cup black rice.
- 2 tablespoons thyme, chopped.
- 1 cup black beans, cooked.
- 4 cups chicken stock.
- A pinch of black pepper.
- Zest of 1/2 lemon, grated.

Procedures:

1. Heat up a pan with the oil over medium-high heat, add the onion, stir and sauté for 6 mins;
2. Add the beans, rice and the other ingredients, toss, bring to a boil and cook over medium heat for 20 mins;
3. Stir the mix, divide between plates and serve it;

Nutrition facts per serving: calories 290 - fat 15.3 - fiber 6.2 - carbs 14.6 - protein 8

Oregano Beans Salad

Preparation time: 10 mins - **Cooking time:** 0 mins - **N. servings:** 4

Ingredients:

- 2 cups black beans, cooked.
- 1 teaspoon oregano, dried.
- 2 tablespoons balsamic vinegar.
- 2 tablespoons olive oil.
- 2 cups white beans, cooked.
- 1 teaspoon basil, dried.
- 1 tablespoon chives, chopped.

Procedures:

1. In a bowl, combine the beans with the vinegar and the other ingredients, toss and serve it as a side dish;

Nutrition facts per serving: calories 322 - fat 15.1 - fiber 10 - carbs 22.0 - protein 7

Avocado Mix

Preparation time: 10 mins - **Cooking time:** 14 mins - **N. servings:** 4

Ingredients:

- 1 teaspoon sweet paprika.
- 1 tablespoon avocado oil.
- 1 pound mixed bell peppers, in strips.
- 1 teaspoon garlic powder.
- Black pepper to the taste.
- 1 avocado, peeled, pitted and halved.
- 1 teaspoon rosemary, dried.
- 1/2 cup veggie stock.

Procedures:

1. Heat up a pan with the oil over medium-high heat, add all the bell peppers, stir and sauté for 5 mins;

2. Add the rest of the ingredients, toss, cook for 10 mins more over medium heat, divide between plates and serve it;

Nutrition facts per serving: calories 245 - fat 13.8 - fiber 5 - carbs 22.5 - protein 5.4

Salmon and Spinach Salad

Preparation time: 10 mins - **Cooking time:** 0 mins - **N. servings:** 4

Ingredients:

- 2 cups smoked salmon, skinless, boneless and cut into strips.
- 1 tablespoon olive oil.
- 1 cup cherry tomatoes, halved.
- 1 tablespoon balsamic vinegar.
- 1 yellow onion, chopped.
- 1 avocado, peeled, pitted and cubed.
- 2 cups baby spinach.
- A pinch of salt and cayenne pepper.

Procedures:

1. In a large salad bowl, mix the salmon with the onion, the avocado and the other ingredients, toss, divide between plates and serve it;

Nutrition facts per serving: calories 260 - fat 2 - fiber 8 - carbs 17 - protein 11

THANK YOU

Thank you for choosing *Italian Home cooking 2021 Vol. 3* for improving your cooking skills! I hope you enjoyed making the recipes as much as tasting them! If you're interested in learning new recipes and new meals to cook, go and check out the other books of the series.